THE IMPERIAL

MACRAMÉ LACE BOOK.

WITH NUMEROUS ILLUSTRATIONS AND INSTRUCTIONS.

FLAX THREADS.

BARBOUR BROTHERS,

No. 134 CHURCH STREET,

NEW YORK.

W. MARTIN, Printer, 47 Murray Street, N. Y.

1877.

INTRODUCTION.

IN introducing this work on Macramé Lace, we are acting in compliance with the wishes of our numerous friends, who are desirous of seeing a fuller development of this interesting study. The subject of Macramé, so well known in ancient times, is now so much in favor that it has already found its way into the principal Courts of Europe, and we take this method of introducing it to the Ladies of America, believing they will find it a fascinating yet simple study.

It is remarkable that this knotted Lace, Macramé, in spite of its ancient date, should have been generally unknown in this country, until we had the honor and privilege of introducing it. Its history goes back to a very early date. Knotted threads in the most ingenious and varied designs may be seen in the pattern books of Tagliente and Il Spechio, between 1530 and 1550.

We have no doubt that as soon as the subject of this beautiful art is understood, it will be taken up and developed by all true lovers of Lace work.

BARBOUR BROTHERS,

134 Church St., New York: 153 Franklin St., Boston,
119 Pine Street, San Francisco.

THREAD WORKS:

HILDEN MILLS, *Lisburn, Ireland.*

BARBOUR FLAX SP'G CO. *Paterson, N. J.*

TRADE MARK.

(From the New York Journal of Commerce, April 9th, 1877.)

A TRIUMPH

—FOR THE—

BARBOUR FLAX SPINNING CO.

(BARBOUR BROTHERS.)

The Philadelphia Exhibition will long be looked upon as the greatest study ever offered to the world. It would seem that the United States desired to unite, in this manifestation of the first centenary of their existence, everything relating to industrial genius and scientific and mechanical progress, and they thus displayed to the eyes of the civilized world so complete a proof of their vitality that it called forth the admiration of both American and foreign visitors.

The French Government, fully alive to this progress and the benefit which might result to our industry by a study of the different branches of manufacture, sent independently of the delegation of intelligent workmen, and their most experienced experts to especially examine the *spinning industry* in this country.

For some years past our European markets have suffered from a decreased exportation to the United States, and this, naturally, has aroused the attention of our French Government. Our celebrated delegate, Mr. Louis Chatel, many of whose observations relating to spinning and weaving in this country we have already reported, expresses himself in the following terms regarding the Linen Threads exhibited by the house of Messrs. BARBOUR BROTHERS, of 134 Church Street, New York.

(Translated from the Reports for the French Government.)

MESSRS. DE MONTAINVILLE AND E. STERNHEIM:

GENTLEMEN:—You request of me information concerning those products whose technical value merits to be signalized in your work of reports to our Government.

On examining the threads and yarns exhibited by Messrs. Barbour Brothers, of New York, the reduction of our exports in these fabrics is explained to me. The perfection in the regularity of their threads is unapproachable, in whatever color they may be dyed.

The raw material used by them is the best European flax, and even in those colors in which the chemical nature of the coloring matter often deteriorates the textile fibre, I have found an extreme resistence of tension. We do not make a better article either in Ireland, or in Scotland, or in France.

Please to receive my sincere, etc.

(Signed.) LOUIS CHATEL.

Member of the French Commission, Philadelphia Exhibition.

It was in consequence of this favorable report that we desired to inform ourselves of the importance of this establishment. But, before entering into details, let us take a general view of this industry and of the causes of its development in this country.

Those industries which are employed in the transformation

of textile substances into thread or woven fabrics constitute one of the most important revenues of modern times. For a great number of years, and up to a recent period, they following a progressive development side by side with other manufacturing productions of prime necessity. Less than fifty years ago the amount of such goods required in the United States could be easily ascertained in advance, since the result was dependent on a population, the consumption by whom was, we may almost say, foreseen, and on means of manufacture which were well ascertained and limited.

Since that time these conditions have been materially altered, for motive powers, called into being by the inventive genius of Americans, have been produced. For the present we will confine ourselves to those causes which have reference solely to the progress made in the manufacture of linen threads for shoemakers and other purposes. We will cite the invention of the sewing machine, which, among its innumerable applications, is to-day the great agent in the rapid manufacture of boots and shoes, and in other work of a similar nature. These machines necessitate the use of a thread which is not only strong, but is above all, even in quality. Hence the development of the industry of linen threads, of which the Messrs. Barbour Brothers are the most important and the best manufacturers in the United States.

The name of BARBOUR is one of the oldest and best known in the linen trade of Belfast, Ireland. It was in 1864, that Messrs. BARBOUR BROTHERS laid the first foundation of their establishment in the United States, which now occupies several acres of ground at Paterson, New Jersey, where they have several buildings, giving employment to six hundred work people. But those having become insufficient, they have now in progress of construction, and nearly finished, additional works on a larger scale, and when these are completed they will employ one thousand work people.

This establishment, as a whole, presents a mechanical completeness which is unrivalled. The spinning rooms contain ten thousand spindles. The machinery is driven by an engine of five hundred horse power. The work rooms, which are large and well ventilated, are constructed in accordance with the best hygienic principles, in view of the large number of work people here congregated. This essential point reflects great credit on the principals of this establishment. Not only have they had every consideration for the comfort of their employees, but the wages are, relatively higher than those paid to our work people in Europe.

These gentlemen buy their raw material in Ireland, France, Belgium and Germany. The first preparations which flax and hemp undergo are partly agricultural and partly manufacturing; but they are imported here in bales, ready for spinning. The orders for these linen threads, which are received, from all parts of the United States, Mexico, China and elsewhere, are all transmitted to the offices of these gentlemen in Church Street, New York.

We do not doubt that Messrs. BARBOUR BROTHERS will send in conjunction with their Belfast house, specimens of their manufactures to our Exposition of Paris in 1878. They will receive a confirmation of the value of their products and of the high appreciation in which they were held by the jury of Philadelphia and by our own experts.

L. C. DE MONTAINVILLE AND E. STERNHEIM.

Originators of the visits to the works and factories on behalf of the Official Delegation of Workmen from the French Government.

MATERIALS FOR MACRAMÉ LACE

AND INSTRUCTIONS.

AN oblong cushion is required, which must be heavy. These look prettiest when made of some bright color, either blue or scarlet, and are best made of silk or Cashmere. The cushion rests on a small table. Two sizes of German pins are also required. The larger size is for pinning on the straight lines at both ends of the cushion, and the small ones are used for putting between the threads on the top line to keep them apart, and fasten the work on to the cushion.

The straight lines may be cut the length of the lace required, and should always be double threads; but if cut too short for the purpose, fresh threads may be joined to those, by tying them together with a weaver's knot. The threads for working should be cut to the exact size given with each pattern; but when the required length is not known, cut the threads a good bit longer than is necessary, and work out one scollop. Then measure how much the fringe is deeper than required, and cut the next threads shorter by so much. The coarse Italian twine is used in making the lace, when intended for furniture, and the finer twine and linen thread, of various sizes for dress trimmings and altar linen. The lace is peculiarly adapted to this latter purpose. The lace also looks beautiful when made of Maltese silk, either in black or bright colors.

The lace is made by knotting threads together. One thread is held firmly over the other as leader, and each single thread is knotted twice on to it. When a leaf is worked from right to left, the leader is held in the left hand, and when a leaf is worked from left to right, the leader is held in the right hand. Pin on as many straight lines as are required for the pattern.

In commencing a pattern, fasten the threads for working on to the top line as follows :--Pass the two ends of each thread under the line, pointing them up, then draw them back through the loop, repeat to the end of the cushion then put in a pin between every four threads, then loosen the second line, hold it firmly in the right hand and knot each thread twice on to it with the left hand. The straight lines are always worked in this way. The Lace as a rule should be worked tightly, as it adds much to its beauty and durability.

No. 1.

A.---Single Chain.

Take two threads, hold one straight in the left hand, knot the other thread on to it once with the right hand; hold this thread straight in the right hand and knot the other on to it with the left. Repeat.

No. 1.

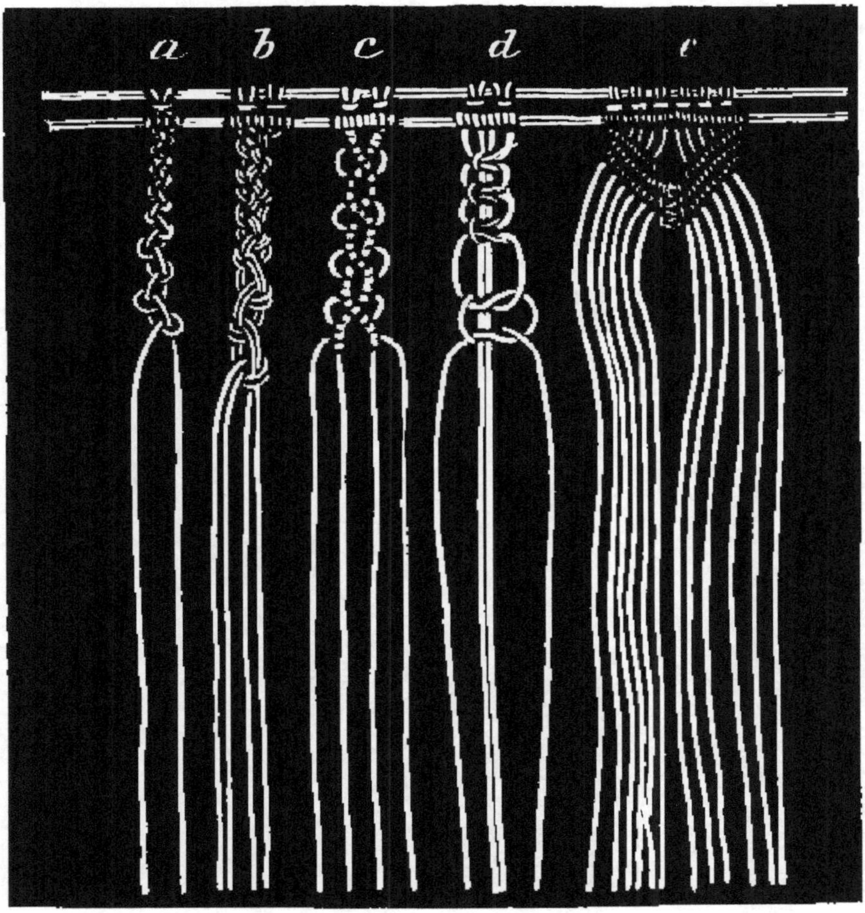

B.—Double Chain.

This is made in the same way as the single chain, but with four threads, using two threads each time instead of one.

C.—Open Chain.

Take four threads commence with the two at the left side, hold the first of these in the right hand as leader, knot the second twice on to it with the left hand, pass the same leader to the left hand, knot the same thread as before twice on to it; take the next two threads, hold the first thread in the right hand as leader, knot the second thread twice on to it, pass the leader to the left hand, knot the same thread as before twice on to it, hold the leader still in the left hand and knot the first leader twice on to it with the right hand; knot the remaining thread at the left side twice on to it, leaving a loop before drawing it up tight.* Pass the same leader back to the right hand, and knot the same thread twice on to it with the left hand. Then take up the two threads at the right side, hold the under one in the right hand, as leader, knot the other thread twice on to it leaving a loop as before. Pass the same leader to the left hand, and knot the same thread twice on to it. Hold the leader still in the left hand and knot the leader at the left side twice on to it;

* It would be well to observe that, in making this open chain, after the loops are made, the leader is always passed into the other hand, and the thread knotted twice on to it.

knot the remaining thread at the left side on to it, leaving a loop as before. Then pass the leader back to the right hand, and knot same thread twice on to it. Repeat from * on preceding page.

D.—Solomon's Knots.

Take four threads, hold the two centre ones straight; pass the thread at left side loosely over these. Take the thread at right side, pass it over the first thread and under the centre ones and up through the loop at left side; draw it up tight. Then take the right-hand thread, pass it over the two centre ones loosely, take the left thread, pass it over this, under the centre ones, and up through the loop at the right side; draw it up tight to meet the first part of the knot. This forms one Solomon's Knot.

E.—Raised Picot.

The Raised Picot mostly comes between two leaves. Take the four centre threads—two from each leaf—hold the two centre ones straight and make six Solomon's knots on to them; pass the two centre threads down through the opening between the two leaves; take one of these threads and knot it once to the thread at the left side, take up the other and knot it once to the remaining thread at the *right side*.

No. 2.

No. 2.

(Threads for this Pattern one yard and two inches long.)

Pin on the straight lines in the usual way, then fasten on the threads to the top line, after which loosen the second line, and knot each thread twice on to it with the left hand. Make a row of Solomon's knots thus :—Take four threads; hold the two centre ones straight, pass the thread at the left side over them loosely, then pass the thread at the right side over this, under the two centre ones, and up through the loop at the left side; draw it up tight. Then pass the right thread over the two centre ones, pass the left thread over this, under the two centre ones, and up through the loop at the right side, draw it up tight to meet the first part of the knot. Repeat to the end of cushion. Then loosen the third line, hold it in the right hand, and knot each thread twice on to it with the left.

First Oval.—*Take eight threads; divide them into two parts. Begin by holding the fourth thread in the left hand as leader, and knot each of the three threads twice on to it with the right; then take the next four threads, hold the first of these in the right hand as leader and knot the three threads on to it with the left hand; then take the two centre threads from each side and make a Solomon's knot; then take the first leader, hold it in the right hand, and knot the three threads on to it; then take the second leader, hold it in the left hand, and knot the seven threads on to it with the right hand. Then divide the eight threads: take the four at the right side, hold the first (at the left side) in the right hand, knot the three threads on to it with the left hand; then take the two centre threads from each side and make a Solomon's knot; then take the leader at the right side, hold it in the left hand, knot three threads on to it; then take the leader at the left side, hold it in the right hand, and knot the remaining three threads on to it with the left hand. Repeat from * to the end of cushion. Then loosen the fourth line, hold it in the right hand, and knot each thread twice on to it with the left hand. Repeat this to the end of the cushion; and for the scollop, take eight threads and repeat from * six times. Then take the top leader from the second oval, hold it in the left hand, and knot the four threads of the first oval on to it with the right hand; then take the top thread at the left side, hold it in the right hand, and knot the three threads of the second oval on to it. Then make a Solomon's knot in the middle with the four centre threads; then take the leader at the left side, hold it in the right hand, and knot three threads on to it with the left; then take the leader at the right side, hold it in the left hand, and knot the four threads on to it with the right. Repeat until there are five small ovals; then make four under these in the same way, and three under the four—and so on—to form the scollop, until it comes to one. If preferred, the fringe may then be knotted, which gives it a rich effect.--See No. 4 Pattern.

No. 3.

(Threads for this Pattern one yard three inches long.)

Pin on the straight lines in the usual way, after which fasten on the threads thus:--Pass the two ends of each thread under the top line, pointing them up, then bring them through the loop, then loosen the second line, hold it in the right hand, and knot each thread twice on to it with the left hand. Then take two threads: hold the first in

No. 3.

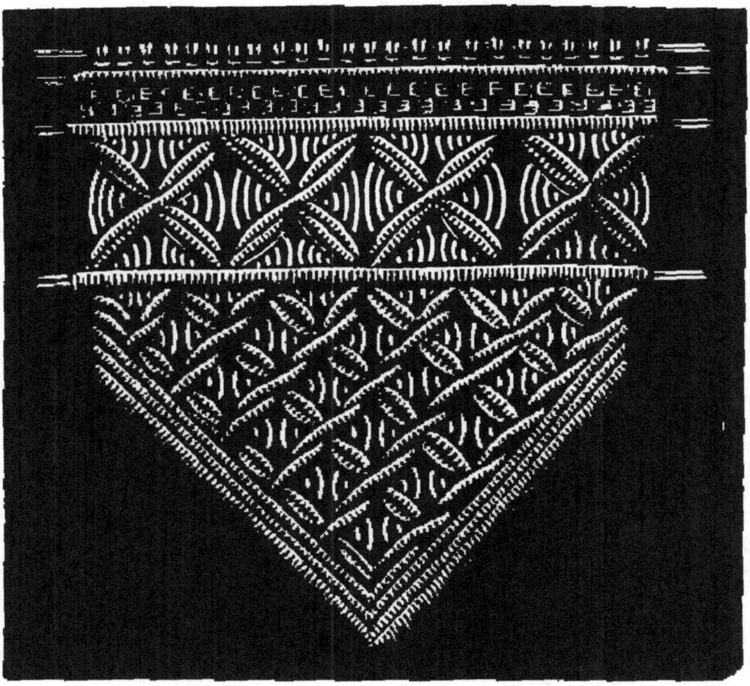

the left hand, knot the other three times on to it with the right hand; repeat this to the end of the cushion. Then take one thread from each: hold one in the right hand, and knot the other on to it with the left hand; repeat to end of cushion. Then loosen the third line at the right side, hold it in the right hand, and knot each thread twice on to it with the left hand. *Take the first six threads, hold the first thread in the right hand as leader, knot the five threads on to it with the left hand, each thread twice; then make the second row of the leaf thus:—Hold the first thread at the left side again in the right hand, knot each of the five threads twice on to it with the left hand; then take the next six threads, hold the sixth thread in the left hand as leader, and knot each of the five threads twice on to it with the right hand; then make the second row of the leaf by holding the sixth thread again in the left hand and knotting each of the five threads on to it with the right; then hold the same thread as leader in the left hand, and knot the leader of the first leaf twice on to it; then make third leaf, hold the same leader still in the left hand, and knot the threads on to it with the right hand; then take the six threads and repeat for a second line; then take the six threads at the right side, hold the first of these (that is the left side one) in the right hand and make the fourth leaf, knotting the threads on with the left hand; repeat for the second line; repeat from * to the end of the cushion; then loosen the fourth line, and knot each thread twice on to it in the usual way.

*For the Scollop.—Take eight threads, divide them into two parts; take the first four threads, hold the first thread in the right hand, and knot the three threads on to it with the left hand. *Second Row of Leaf.*—Take the first thread again, hold it in the right hand and knot the three threads on with the left hand; then take the next four threads, hold the fourth thread as leader in the feft hand, and knot each of the three threads on to it with the right. Make the second row of the leaf in the same way; hold the leader still in the left hand, and join the two leaves by knotting the leader of the first leaf twice on to it. Repeat from * six times, then reduce it one in each row until the point is formed according to the engraving; then join the two leaders of the leaves at the point; then take the first thread at the left side, hold it in the right hand as leader, and knot each thread three times on to it down the side of the scollop to form a continuous line; then take the thread at right side of the scollop, hold it in the left hand, and knot each thread three times on to it with the right hand; then join the two leaders by holding one tight and knotting the other twice on to it; then take the first thread again at the left side and make a second line, after which take the first thread at the right side, hold it in the left hand and make a second line; repeat at each side to form a third line. The leader is always held at the top, and the threads underneath, after which the threads are all held back, fastened down with a needle and thread on the wrong side, and then cut close.

No. 4.

(Threads for this Pattern to be one yard long.)

Commence by pinning on the straight lines in the usual way, after which fasten on the threads for working, to the top or first line. Pass the two ends of each thread under the line, pointing them up, then draw them through the loop; then loosen the second line at the right side, and knot each thread twice on to it with the left hand.

No. 4.

Then make a row of Solomon's knots with every four threads to the end, after which loosen the third line, and knot the threads on to it as before. Then take four threads and make three Solomon's knots with them. Repeat to the end of the cushion. Then loosen the fourth line, and knot each thread twice on to it with the left hand as before; then take the first four threads, hold the first of these in the right hand as leader at the top, and knot the three threads on to it with the left (each thread twice); then pass the same leader to the left hand, and knot each of the three threads on to it with the right. Repeat this five times. Then make two more chains, exactly the same as last. Then take six threads: hold the first in the right hand as leader (the leader should always be at top, and the threads underneath), and make a leaf of two rows; then take the next six threads, hold the one at the right side in the left hand as leader, and make a leaf of two rows; then take the two centre threads of each leaf, and with them make a row of six Solomon's knots; then pass the two centre threads of these four between the two leaves, pointing them down, and knot these threads to the other two, to form the raised Picot. Then take the centre thread at the left side, hold it in the left hand as leader, and knot the threads on with the right hand, to make the lower leaf at the left side (two rows); then take the centre thread at the right side, hold it in the right hand as leader, and make the lower leaf at the right side; then make three more chains, and then another star of four leaves, with raised Picot in the centre. Repeat to the end of cushion. Loosen the fifth line, and knot each thread twice on to it, as before. Take four threads, make three Solomon's knots with these. Repeat to the end of cushion. Loosen the sixth line, and knot each thread twice on to it as before; then make a row of Solomon's knots with every four threads; then loosen the seventh line and knot each thread twice on to it, as before.

To finish off the Insertion.--Keep the last line pinned on at both ends; take two threads, draw the second one up under the line in a loop, pass the ends of both threads through this loop, draw them up tight, to form a knot, same as the one at the top line. The the two threads will now be in front, between the two last lines. Pass these threads to the back, one at each side of the knot, tie them firmly together at the back; sew these threads neatly to the work, on the wrong side, with a needle and thread. Repeat to the end of cushion, and then cut the threads close.

No. 5.

(Threads for this Pattern one yard and four inches long.)

Pin on the straight lines in the usual way, and fasten on the threads for working as described in the former patterns. Loosen the second line, and knot each thread twice on to it to the end of the cushion. Take the first four threads, hold three in the right hand and knot the first thread twice over them with the left hand; repeat to the end of the cushion. Loosen the third line, and knot each thread twice on to it as usual. * Take eight threads, hold the first as leader in the right hand, and knot each of the seven threads twice on to it with the left hand; then divide these eight threads into two parts; take the first four of these threads, hold three in the left hand, and knot the fourth thread twice over them with the right hand; do the same to the next four threads; then take the first of these threads, hold it in the right hand and knot each of the seven threads twice on to it with the left hand. The second and third leaves are made in the same way. *Fourth Leaf*--Take the eighth

knotted sixteen times, increase two in each to the centre; then begin at the left side, take up the sixteen threads, leave out two of them, hold the next thread in the right hand as leader, and knot each thread twice on to it; also knot on the two threads of the first single chain to it; then repeat the knotting up of every four threads after which make another long line, leaving out the two first threads, and knotting on the two threads of the second chain; repeat this until there are five long rows; then leave out four threads in the two following rows; then make a row with eight threads, and to finish the end of the scollop make four close lines according to the engravings. Repeat for the right hand side of the scollop, holding the leaders in the left hand, and knotting the threads on with the right hand. The last three rows at the end of scollop are joined together, the threads are then knotted to make a knotted fringe.

No. 6.

(Threads for this Pattern one yard and three quarters long.)

Pin on the straight lines in the usual way, and fasten the threads for working on to the top line; then loosen the second line, hold it in the right hand, and knot each thread twice on to it. Take the first four threads, make three Soloman's knots with them; repeat to the end of the cushion. Take the fourth * row of Solomon's knots, divide the four threads into two parts, make five single chains with the two first threads, and eight single chains with the other two threads; then take the eighth row of Solomon's knots, and make six single chains with each two threads. Take the first thread at the left side, hold it in the right hand as leader, and knot eleven threads on

No. 6.

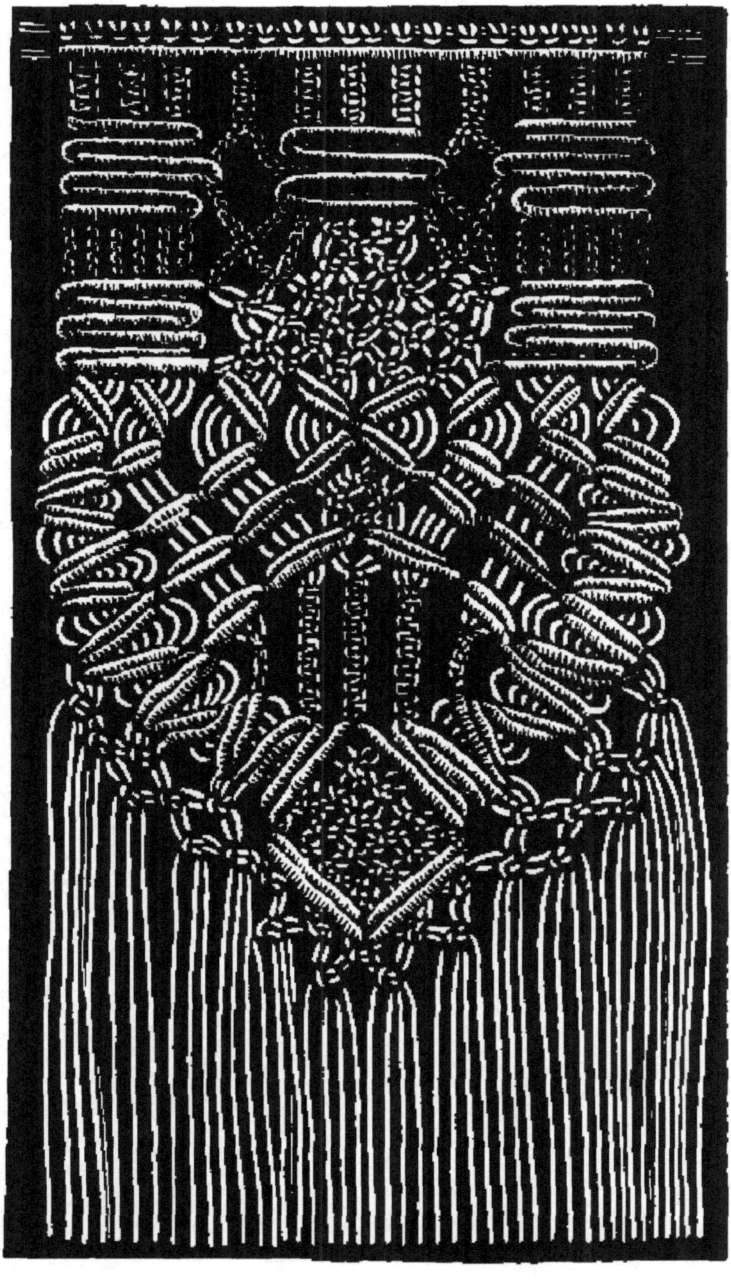

to it ; then pass the leader to the left hand, and knot the same threads on to it with the right hand ; then pass the same leader back to the right hand, and knot the threads on to it with the left, also the two threads of the first single chain. Pass the leader again to the left hand, and knot the threads on to it with the right ; pass the leader back to the right hand, and knot the same threads on to it with the left, leaving out the two last threads, which are to be knotted in single chain six times ; then pass the leader to the left hand, and knot the same threads on to it with the right. Divide these threads into six parts, and make eight single chains with every two threads. Commence at the seventh row of Solomon's knots; take the thread at the right side, hold it in the left hand, and knot eleven threads on to it with the right hand. Divide those twelve threads into six parts, and make two single chains with every two threads. Then pass the thread at the left side to the right hand, and knot each thread twice on to it with the left hand, and also the two threads of the next single chain. Then make another row of single chain. Then pass the same leader back to the left hand, and knot each thread twice on to it, also the threads of the second chain ; pass the same leader to the right hand, and knot each thread twice on to it with the left ; repeat from * to the end of the cushion. Take the two threads at each end of the centre pattern, and make six single chains on each. Make two Solomon's knots with the eight middle threads; make a Solomon's knot under these, taking two threads from each knot ; make a Solomon's knot at each side, and then one in the centre, and so on, according to the engraving.

And now, having clearly described the pattern so far, the rest may be easily copied from the engraving by any worker who has followed the directions to this stage.

The scollop being composed of leaves, with very little variety, the instructions for it would be only a repetition of any of the former patterns.

No. 7.

(Threads for this Pattern to be one and a half yards long.)

Pin on the lines in the usual way, after which fasten on the threads for working; then loosen the second line, hold it in the right hand, and knot each thread twice on to it with the left. Take four threads, hold the three first ones in the left hand, knot the fourth thread three times over them with the right. Repeat to the end of cushion. Take two threads from each, hold three in the right hand and knot the first thread three times over them with the left. Repeat to end of cushion. Then loosen the third line, hold it in the right hand, and knot each thread twice over it with the left hand. * Take eight threads, make a Solomon's knot with the first four, hold the eighth thread in the left hand as leader, and knot each thread twice on to it with the right hand, take the eighth thread again as leader, and make a second row same as the last; take the next eight threads, make a Solomon's knot with the last four, then take the first thread, hold it as leader in the right hand, and knot each of the seven threads twice on to it with the left hand. Then take the eight threads again, and make a second row; then make eight Solomon's knots with those threads. After this, take the first thread at the left side, hold it in the right hand as leader, and knot each of the seven threads twice on to it with the left hand. Repeat for a second line. Then take the thread at the right side, hold it in

No. 7.

the left hand as leader, and knot each thread twice on to it. Repeat for a second line. Take the first four threads, make a Solomon's knot the same with last four threads. Then take the next four threads, hold two in each hand, and make twelve double chain, make two more rows of double chain. Repeat from * to the end of cushion. Then loosen the fourth line, hold it in the right hand and knot each thread twice on to it with the left hand. Then take the first four threads, and make a Solomon's knot. Repeat to the end of cushion. Loosen the fifth line, hold it in the right hand, and knot each thread twice on to it with the left. * Take six threads, hold the first in the right hand as leader, and knot the five threads on to it with the left. Repeat for two more lines. Take the next six threads, hold the sixth in the left hand, and knot the five threads on to it with the right hand. Repeat for two more lines; then make a raised Picot with the four centre threads, then take the centre thread at the left side, hold it in the left hand, and knot the five threads on to it. Repeat for two more lines. Take the centre thread at the right side, hold it in the right hand, and knot the five threads on to it with the left hand. Repeat for two more lines; then take the next four threads, and make a row of open chain as described in diagram C, then repeat with the next four threads. Repeat from * to the end of cushion. Then loosen the sixth line, hold it in left hand, and knot each thread twice on to it. Take the first four threads, make a Solomon's knot. Repeat to the end of cushion; loosen the seventh line, hold it in the right hand, and knot each thread twice on to it. The next part of the insertion is made exactly like the first, and to finish off keep the last line pinned on at both ends, take two threads, draw the second one up under the line in a loop, then pass the ends of both threads through this loop, draw them up tight to form a knot, same as the one at the top line; the two threads will then be in front, between the last two lines, pass these threads to the back one at each side of the knot, tie the two threads firmly together at the back, sew them neatly down on the wrong side, repeat to the end of cushion, and cut off the threads close.

No. 8.

(Threads for this Pattern one yard and nine inches long.)

Pin on the stright lines or leaders to the cushion; then fasten on the threads to the top line, so:—Take a thread; pass the two ends of it under the line, pointing them up, and then bring them down through the loop. Loosen the second leader by taking out the pin at the right side, hold it in the right hand and knot each thread twice on to it with the left hand. Take the first four threads, and with them make three Solomon's knots. (These knots are made as follows:—Take four threads, hold the two centre ones straight, pass the thread at the left side loosely over these; then take the thread at the right side, pass it over the first thread, under the centre ones, and up through the loop at the left side; draw it up tight, then take the right hand thread, pass it over the two centre ones loosely; take the left thread, pass it over this, under the centre ones, and up through the loop at the right side, draw it up tight to meet the first part of the knot). Repeat to end of the cushion. Then loosen the third line by taking out the pin at the right side, hold it in right hand, and knot each thread twice on to it with the left hand. To make the first leaf:—Take eight threads, hold the first one in the right hand, over the others, and knot each

No. 7.

of the seven threads twice on to it with the left hand. Take the first thread again, hold it in the right hand, and knot the threads on to it as before. Take the next eight threads, hold the eighth one in the left hand, and knot each of the seven threads twice on to it with the right hand. Take the eighth thread again, hold it in the right hand, and knot the seven threads on to it, as before. Then make a raised Picot, so:—Take the two centre threads of each leaf, and with these four threads make six Solomon's knots; then pass the two centre threads between the two leaves, pointing them down; then knot each of these threads on the two remaining ones, to fasten them; then take the eighth thread, hold it in the left hand, and knot each of the seven threads twice on to it with the right hand; take the eighth thread again, hold it in the left hand, and knot each of the seven threads on to it, as before. Then take the next thread to make the fourth leaf, hold it in the right hand, knot each of the seven threads twice on to it with the left hand; take up the thread again, hold it in the right hand, and knot each of the seven threads on to it, as before. This forms the first star. Repeat to end of cushion. Loosen the fourth line, hold it in the right hand, and knot each thread on to it with the left hand.

The Scollop.—As the scollop is made of these stars, it is not necessary to describe them further; and to finish the scollop when the stars are all made, take the first thread, hold it in the right hand, and knot each thread twice on to it; but when the stars meet, knot two of the threads three times, instead of twice—this makes the straight line more even, and joins the stars more completely; then take the first thread at the right side of the scollop, hold it in the left hand, and do the same. Repeat at the right side, then at the left side; then take the ninth thread at the left side, hold it in the right hand, and knot the threads on to it with the left hand.

Repeat at the right side. Then take the seventeenth thread, hold it in the right hand, and knot the remaining threads on to it with the left hand. Repeat at the right side, to finish the scollop.

No. 9.

(Threads for this Pattern one yard and eighteen inches long.)

Pin on three straight lines, and fasten the threads for working on to the top line in the usual way; then take the pin out of the second line at the right side, hold it in the right hand, and knot each thread twice on to it with the left hand. Repeat with the third line. Take the first four threads, and with them make four Solomon's knots. Repeat to the end of the cushion. Then take the first four threads; hold the fourth in the right hand, and knot the first thread of the next four twice on to it; then take the second thread of the second four, hold it in the left hand, and knot two threads of the first four on to it; then take the second thread of the first four, hold it in the right hand, and knot three threads of the second four on to it with the left hand; then take the third thread of the second four, hold it in the left hand, and knot three threads of the first four on to it; then take the first thread of the first four, hold it in the right hand, and knot the four threads on to it; then take the fourth thread of the second four, hold it in the left hand, and knot the four threads on to it from the other side—this completes the diamond. Repeat to the end of cushion.

The scollop is formed by leaving out a diamond in each row, until only one diamond remains.

No. 8.

No. 10.

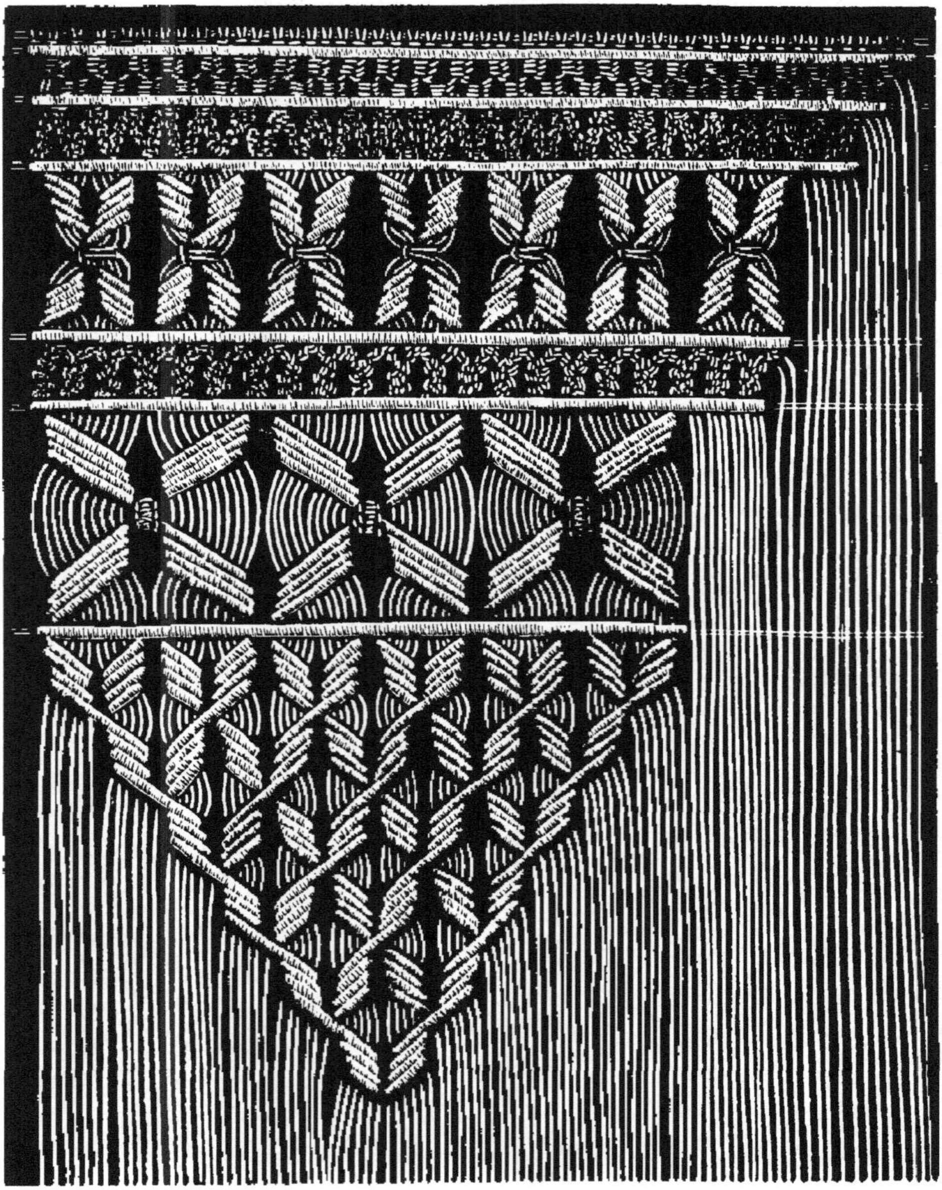

No. 10.

(Threads for this Pattern two yards three inches long.)

Pin on the straight lines or leaders to the cushion in the usual way, then fasten the threads for working on to the top line. Loosen the second line at the right side by taking out the pin which confines it to the cushion; hold the leader in the right hand and knot each thread twice on to it with the left; take the first four threads, hold three in the left hand, and knot the fourth thread three times over them with the right hand. Repeat to the end of cushion. Then take the first two threads, hold the first in the left hand and knot the other three times over it with the right hand; then take the next four threads, hold three of them in the left hand, and knot the fourth thread three times over them with the right hand. Repeat to the end of cushion. Then loosen the third line; hold it in the right hand, and knot each thread twice on to it with the left; then take the first four threads, make a Solomon's knot. Repeat to the end. Take the first two threads and make four single chain, as follows:—Hold the first thread straight in the left hand, knot the other thread on to it with the right hand; then hold this thread straight in the right hand, knot the other on to it with the left; hold this thread in the left hand, knot the other on to it with the right; hold this in the right hand, and knot the other on with the left; take the next two threads, do the same, and repeat with every two threads to the end of cushion; then miss the first two threads, and with the next four threads make a Solomon's knot. Repeat to the end. Then loosen the fourth line, hold it in the right hand and knot each thread twice on to it with the left. For the first leaf take six threads ; hold the first as leader in the right hand over the others, and knot each of the five threads twice on to it with the left hand ; then take the first thread again, hold it as before in the right hand, and knot each of the five threads twice on to it with the left. Repeat for two more rows. This forms the first leaf. For the second leaf :—Take six threads ; hold the sixth in the left hand over the others, and knot each thread on to it with the right hand. Repeat three more times. Then take the outside thread at each side and make a Solomon's knot with these over all the ten threads ; then divide the twelve threads, and hold the sixth thread in the left hand, and knot the other five threads on to it with the right hand. Repeat three times more ; and for the fourth leaf :—Take the first thread of the remaining six threads ; hold it in the right hand, and knot each of the five threads twice on to it with the left. Repeat three times more ; this finishes the star of four leaves. Repeat to the end of cushion ; then loosen the fifth line, hold it in the right hand, and knot each thread twice on to it with the left. Then take the first four threads, make a Solomon's knot. Repeat to the end. Then take two threads from each Solomon's knot, and with these make four double chain. This is made same as single, only holding two threads in each hand instead of one. Then loosen the sixth line hold it in the right hand, and knot each thread twice on to it with the left ; then take twelve threads, hold the first in the right hand, and knot each of the eleven threads on to it with the left. Repeat three times more. This forms the first large leaf. Then take the next twelve threads ; hold the twelfth in the left hand, and knot each of the eleven threads on to it with the right. Repeat three times more. This forms the second leaf. Then take the four centre threads, and with them make a raised Picot (this is described in Pattern No. 1) ; then divide these twenty-four threads into two parts; hold the twelfth thread in the left hand, and knot each thread of the eleventh twice on to it with the right. Repeat three times more; and for the fourth leaf:—Hold the first thread of the twelve in the right hand, and knot each of the others twice on to it with the left. Repeat three times more. This forms the star of four large leaves. Repeat to the end. Loosen the seventh line. hold it in the right hand, and knot each thread twice on to it with the left.

To Make the Scollop.—Take six threads; hold the first thread in the right hand, and knot the other five threads twice on to it with the left. Repeat three times more. This forms the first leaf. Then take the next six threads; hold the sixth thread in the left hand, and knot the other five threads on to it with the right hand. Repeat three times more. Join the leaders of both these together, by holding one straight, and knot the other twice over it; then take the next six threads, hold the first thread in the right hand, and knot each of the five threads twice on to it. Repeat three times more to form the leaf. Then take the next six threads, hold the sixth thread in the left hand, and knot the others twice on to it with the right. Repeat three times more. When this leaf is finished hold the leader still in the left hand, and knot six threads twice on to it. Repeat three times more to form the leaf. Then take the six threads that were used in making the second leaf of the scollop; hold the first of these in the right hand, and knot each thread twice on to it with the left. Repeat three times more for the leaf. Then join the leader of this leaf to the leader of the leaf next to it. Repeat till the scollop is completed.

No. 11.

(Threads for this Pattern one yard and twenty-seven inches long.)

Pin on the lines to the cushion in the usual way, after which fasten the threads for working on to the top line. Loosen the second line, hold it in the right hand, and knot each thread twice on to it with the left; then loosen the next line and do the same. Then * take the first four threads, make a Solomon's knot; then with the first two of these threads make four single chain; with the other two threads make three single chain. Then take the next four threads, hold the first three of these in the left hand, and knot the fourth thread four times over them. Then to make the small Picot, make a running knot with the fourth thread, draw it up close to the work, then make another knot in the same way, but let it come inside the first knot, quite close to the work; then with the same thread make four more knots over the three threads. Then take these four threads, and the two threads of the single chain close to it, and with the six threads make a Solomon's knot; then take the first four of these, and the two threads of the first single chain, and with the six threads make another Solomon's knot; then take the first four of these threads, hold three of them in the right hand, and knot the first thread four times over them with the left hand; then make a small Picot; after which make four more knots with the same thread over the three threads; then take the next four threads, make eight knots with those, each knot being the first part of the Solomon's knot. This makes a twist. Then take the next four threads, and with them make six knots in the same way. Take the next four threads and make eight knots of the same. Then

No. 11.

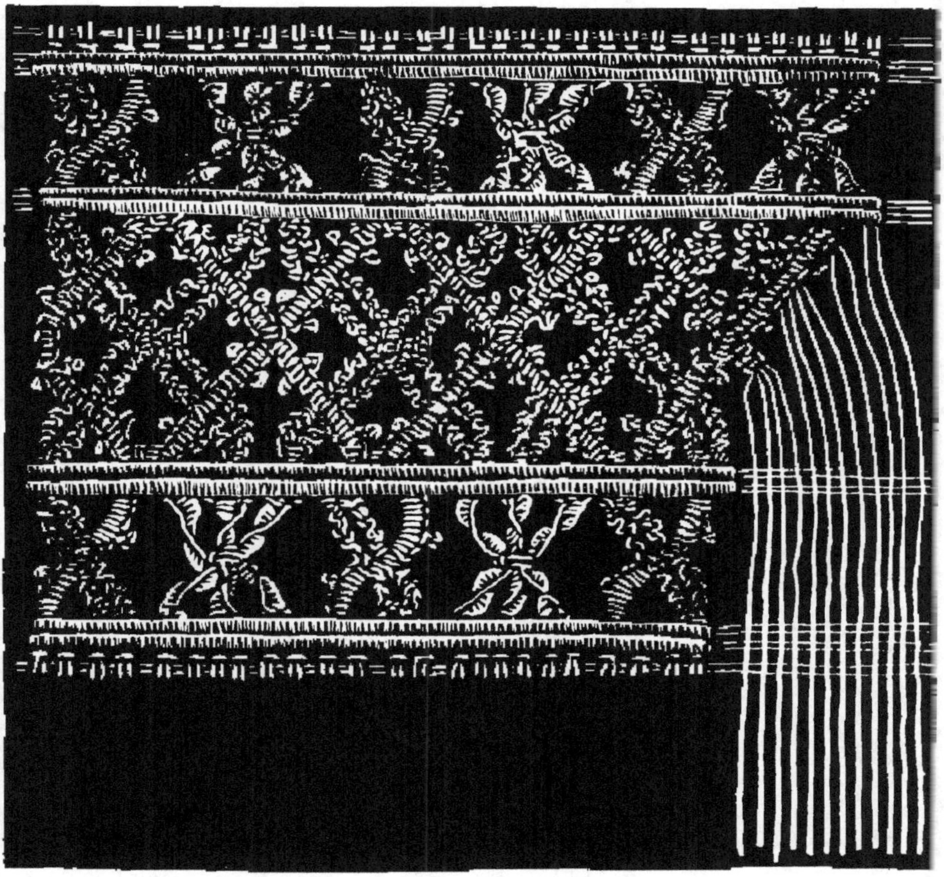

take these twelve threads, hold the ten centre threads together, and make a Solomon's knot over them with the two outside threads Then take the first four of these threads, make eight knots same as before. Take the next four threads, make six knots Take the next four threads, make eight of the same knots. Repeat from * to the end of cushion. Loosen the fourth line, hold it in the right hand, and knot each thread twice on to it with the left. Loosen the next line and do the same. Then take the first four threads, make a Solomon's knot; take the first two of these four threads and make six single chain; take the next two threads, make four chain; miss the next two threads, and with the next four threads make a Solomon's knot. Then take two of these threads and the two threads that were missed, and with them make a Solomon's knot; then make another; then make a small Picot at each side; then make another Solomon's knot with the same threads. Then take these four threads, and the two threads of the single chain close to it, and with the six threads make a Solomon's knot. Then leave out two threads at the right side, and make a Solomon's knot with the four threads. Then take in the two threads of the first single chain, and with the six threads make a Solomon's knot; then leave out two threads at the right side again, and with the four threads make a Solomon's knot; then make a small Picot at each side; then make three more Solomon's knots; then a small Picot at each side; then another Solomon's knot; then take two of the threads that were left out, and with them make four single chain; then take the other two threads and make four single chain; then take the two threads left at the top Solomon's knot and the two threads next to it, and make a Solomon's knot; then make another; then a small Picot at each side; then another Solomon's knot; then take four threads, make a Solomon's knot; then take the first two of these threads, make four single chain; then make a Solomon's knot with these two threads and the four threads next to it; then leave out two threads at the left side, and make a Solomon's knot with the four threads; then with the two top threads make six single chain; then with these two threads, and the four threads close to them, make a Solomon's knot; then take the four threads at the left side, and make four single chain with the first two, and six single chain with the next two; then make a Solomon's knot with the four threads; then take two of these threads, and two from the knot at the left side of them, and with them make a Solomon's knot; then make a Solomon's knot with the four threads at the left side; then make a Solomon's knot with the four threads at the right side; then make a Solomon's knot with the four centre threads: then make a Solomon's knot with the four threads at the left side; then make four single chain with the first two threads, and four single chain with the other two threads; then make a Solomon's knot with the two threads of the first chain and the four threads close to them; then with the first two threads at the left side make six chain, and make a Solomon's knot with the four threads at the right; then take the two threads of the chain at the right side, and the four threads close to them, and with the six threads make a Solomon's knot. Take the first two of these threads and make four single chain; then, with these two threads, and the two close to them at the right side, make a Solomon's knot. This brings the centre pattern close to the fifth line; and when the centre pattern is made to the end of cushion, loosen the sixth line, and knot each thread twice on to it. Loosen the next line and do the same; then for the next part repeat from *.

To finish off the Insertion.—Keep the last line pinned

No. 12.

on at both ends. Take two threads; draw the second one up under the line in a loop; pass the ends of both threads through this loop; draw them up tight, to form a knot same as the one at the top line. The two threads will now be in front between the two last lines; pass these threads to the back one at each side of the knot; tie them firmly together at the back; sew these threads neatly to the work on the wrong side with a needle and thread. Repeat to the end of cushion, and then cut the threads close.

No. 12.

(Threads for this Pattern two yards and eighteen inches long.)

Pin on the lines to the cushion, after which fasten the threads for working on to the top line. Loosen the next line, hold it in the right hand, and knot each thread twice on to it with the left hand. * Take the first three threads; hold two in the right hand and knot the first thread four times over it with the left hand; then leave a little loop, so:—put a pin between the last knot, and the one now being made; then make four more knots. Take the next three threads; hold two in the left hand, and knot the fourth thread eight times over them with the right hand, leaving a loop in the middle same as at the other side. Then to join them, take two threads at from each and make one plain knot: then take the three threads at the left side, hold two in the right hand and knot the first thread eight times over them, leaving the little loop in the middle. Then take the other three threads; hold two in the left hand, knot the third thread eight times over them with the right, leaving a loop in the middle. Then take the next four threads ; hold the first thread in the right hand, knot the three threads over it with the left. Repeat again to make a leaf. Take the next four threads ; hold the fourth thread in the left hand, knot the three threads over it with the right hand. Repeat again. Hold the same leader still in the left hand, and knot the four threads from the left side on to it with the right hand. Repeat again. Then take the other four threads ; hold the first of them in the right hand, knot the three threads on to it with the left hand. Repeat again. Repeat from * to the end of cushion. Loosen the third line, hold it in the right hand, knot each thread twice on to it with the left hand. Miss the first two threads; take the next two threads, make three single chain ; take the next two, make four single chain ; take the next two, make six single chain ; take the next two, make eight single chain ; take the next two threads, make nine single chain. There will now be twelve threads. Take the first thread ; hold it in the right hand, and knot each of the eleven threads twice on to it with the left hand. Repeat for two more rows. Take the first four of these threads ; hold the fourth in the left hand, and make a leaf of two rows ; pass the leader into the right hand, and make a leaf of two rows. Leave those for the present. Take the next two threads of the twelve ; make eight single chain. Take the next thread of the twelve ; hold it in the right hand, and knot each of the remaining threads on to it with the left. This part is left for the present. Take up the next six threads ; miss the first two ; with the next two make three single chain ; with the next two make five single chain ; then take the first of the two that were missed, hold it in the right hand and knot each of the five threads on to it with the left. Repeat for two more rows. Take the next two threads ; make five single chain ; make three single chain with the next two threads. Take two more threads; hold the second in the left hand, and knot each of the five threads on to it with the left. Repeat for two more rows.

Having described this in detail so far, it is not necessary to continue, as it would be only a repetition of the same thing, and at this stage it would be calculated more to puzzle the worker. The best thing now is to follow the engraving, and when the centre part is made, loosen the fourth line, hold it in the right hand, and knot each thread twice on to it with the left hand.

To Make the Scollop.—Count off eighteen threads; this will be the centre of scollop. Count off eighteen threads for the other side of the scollop. Take the two centre threads at the left side, make six single chain; take the next two at the left side, make three chain; take the next two, hold the first in the right hand as leader, and knot each of the five threads on to it twice with the left hand. Repeat for two more rows. Then with six threads from the other side of the scollop do exactly the same, only this time holding the leader in the left hand, and knotting the threads on to it with the right hand; join the two leaders together by holding one, and knotting the other over it twice. Then there will be twelve threads, with every two of these make three single chain. Then take up the next two threads at the left side; hold the second thread in the right hand, aad knot the first thread twelve times on to it with the left hand, leaving a loop in the middle by inserting a pin between the threads; then hold the under thread of those two in the right hand as leader, and knot six threads twice on to it with the left. Repeat for two more rows. Then take up the two threads at the other side of the scollop, and do exactly the same, working towards the centre of the scollop. When the third row is made, take four threads at the left side; hold the first in the right hand, knot three threads each twice over it; take four threads at the right side; hold the fourth in the left hand; knot each thread twice on to it with the right hand; join in the middle. Repeat the same at left side. Repeat at right side, until there are five rows, all joined in the middle. Take the first four threads, hold three in the right hand; knot the first thread ten times over them with the left; this will form a thick strand. Do the same at the right side. There are now four threads left at each side from the leaf; take the first two of these, and make seven single chain; make ten with the other two; do the same at the right side. Then commence at the top of the scollop again; left side, take two threads, make six single chain; with the next two make four single chain, and three with the next two. Then take the next two threads; hold the first of these in the right hand; knot seven threads twice on to it with the left hand. Repeat for two more rows. Then take the next two threads, which will be the outside ones; hold the second in the right hand, and knot the first thread ten times on to it with the left hand, leaving a loop in the centre. Take one of these threads; hold it in the right hand as leader, and knot eight threads twice on to it; with the left hand then take up the other thread, which is the last one left; hold it in the right hand; and knot nine threads twice on to it with the left. Then leave out the first four threads. Take the next thread, hold it in the right hand; knot each thread twice on to it with the left, taking in the first chain. Repeat for two more rows. Miss the first four threads; take the next thread, hold it in the right hand; knot each thread twice on to it with the left, taking in the second single chain. Repeat for two more rows. Miss the first four threads; take up the next thread, hold it in the right hand, knot each thread twice on to it with the left hand, taking in the thick strand. Repeat

No. 13.

for two more rows. Miss the first four threads; take up the next thread, hold it in the right hand, knot each thread twice on to it with the left hand. Repeat for two more rows. Leave out four threads again, and with the other four make a strand, so:—Hold three threads in the right hand and knot the first one eight times over it with the left; then take the first four threads that were left out, hold the first in the right hand, knot the three threads each twice on to it with the left hand. Repeat for two more rows. This forms a small leaf; do exactly the same with each four threads that were left out, there will then be five leaves. Take the first leaf, hold three of its threads in the right hand, knot the first thread twelve times over them with the left hand, leaving a loop in the centre of them. Then take the four threads of the next leaf and the four threads of the first; hold seven of these threads in the left hand and knot the first on to them with the left three times, then cut away two threads closely at the back of the work; then knot on the same thread until there are twelve knots, leaving a loop in the centre. Repeat until all the five leaves are worked in. Do exactly the same thing at the right hand side of the scollop, and to finish it at the point, take the six threads left, three from each side, let tnem cross one over the other, and knot one thread neatly over them drawing very tight, and cut off the threads at the back, and fasten neatly with a needle and fine thread.

No. 13.

(Threads for this Pattern one yard and four inches long.)

Pin on the straight lines in the usual way to the cushion; then fasten the threads for working on to the top line. Then loosen the second line at the right side, hold it in the right hand, and knot each thread twice on to it with the left. * Take three threads ; hold two in the left hand, and knot the third thread twice over them with the right. Repeat to the end of cushion. Leave out the first thread, take up the next three threads; hold the first two in the left hand, knot the third thread twice over them with the right. Repeat to the end of cushion. Loosen the third line, hold it in the right hand, knot each thread twice on to it with the left hand. Take the first four threads; hold the fourth thread in the left hand, and knot each of the three threads twice on to it with the right; pass the same leader to the right hand, knot the threads on with the left, pass the leader back to the left hand, knot the threads on with the right, pass the leader again to the right hand, knot the threads on with the left. This will make four twists. Take the next four threads, make three twists in the same way; take the next four threads. make two twists ; take the next four threads, hold the fourth thread in the left hand, and knot all the fifteen threads each twice on to it with the right hand. Repeat for another row; leave this for the present. Take the next four threads ; hold the fourth thread in the right hand, knot each of the three threads twice on to it with the right, then pass the leader to the right hand. Repeat to make four twists. Then take four threads at the left side, make a twist of three; take the next four threads, make a twist of three; take the next four threads at the left side, and again make a twist of three; leave this. Commence at the top, miss four threads, take up the next four threads, and with them make a twist of two; take the next four threads, make a twist of three; take the next four threads, make a twist of four, then go back to the four threads that were missed; take the first of these, hold it in the right hand, knot the fifteen threads each twice on to it with the left. Repeat for a second line. Leave out the four threads

No. 14.

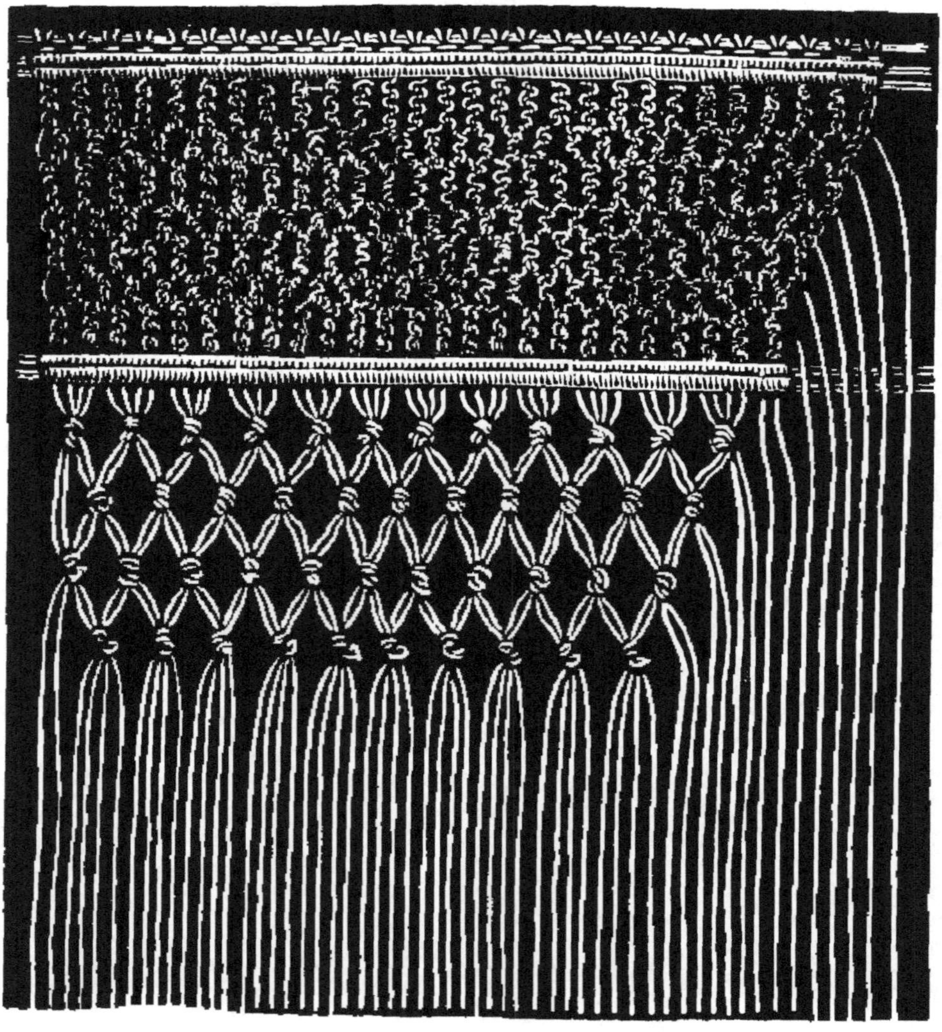

of these at the right side, and with the next four threads make a twist of three; with the next four threads do the same, and the same with the next four threads; then take up one of the centre threads of the middle twist, hold it in the hand, and knot nine threads at the left hand side on to it with the right hand; then take up again the centre thread of the middle twist, hold it in the right hand, and knot each of the nine threads on to it with the left; then take six threads from each side, hold eight in the middle, and make a Solomon's knot with the two from each side, this forms half the diamond, and for the lower half repeat the instructions for the above; reversing them. Repeat to the end of cushion. Then loosen the fourth line, hold it in the right hand, and knot each thread twice on to it with the left. Repeat from *; after which loosen the fifth line, hold it in the right hand, and knot each thread twice on to it with the left. For the fringe take six threads, and with them make a running knot. Repeat to the end.

No. 14.

(Threads for this Pattern one yard long.)

Pin the straight lines on to the cushion in the usual way; then fasten on the threads for working to the top line. Then loosen the second line, hold it in the right hand, and knot each thread twice on to it with the left. Repeat for another row. Take the first two threads; make four single chain. Repeat to the end of cushion. Miss the first thread and with the two next threads make two single chain. Repeat to the end of cushion. Take the first two threads; make four single chain; repeat. Miss the first thread, and with the next two threads make two chain. Repeat to the end of cushion. Take the first two threads; make four chain. Repeat to end of cushion. Miss the first thread with the next two threads; make two chain; Repeat to end of cushion. Take the first two threads; make four chain. Repeat to end of cushion. Then loosen the fourth straight line, hold it in the right hand, knot each thread twice over it; loosen the next straight line, hold it in the right hand, knot each thread twice on to it with the left; and for the fringe, take four threads and with them make a running knot, draw it up to within a quarter of an inch of the last straight line. Repeat to end of cushion. Miss the two first threads; make a similar knot with the next four threads. Repeat to end of cushion. Make two more rows of knots.

This makes a handsome fringe, and is especially adapted for silk.

No. 15.

(Threads for this Pattern one yard and twenty-seven inches long.)

Pin the straight lines on to the cushion in the usual way, and fasten the threads for working on to the top line. Loosen the second line, hold it in the right hand, knot each thread twicc on it. Take the first four threads; make two double chain. Repeat to the end. Then loosen the third line, hold it in the right hand, knot each thread twice on to it with the left hand. Take three threads; hold the first thread in the right hand, knot two on to it with the left hand; take the next three threads, hold the third in the left hand,

No. 15.

knot three on to it with the right hand; take the first thread, hold it in the right hand; knot three threads on to it with the left. Repeat at each side, until there are five rows to each leaf; then take the six threads, make a Solomon's knot, repeat to the end of cushion. Loosen the fourth line, hold it in the right hand, knot each thread twice on to it with the left. Take the first two threads, with them make five single chain. Take the next four threads; hold the fourth thread in the left hand, knot the three threads twice over it. Take the next four, hold the fourth in the left hand, knot each of the nine threads over it with the right; repeat for two more rows. Take the first two of these threads. Make four chain; make three chain with all the other threads; leave those for the present. Take four threads; make a Solomon's knot; take two of these threads, make four single chain; do the same with the other two threads. Take the first of these four threads; hold it in the left hand, knot eight threads over it with the right hand; take the next of the four threads, hold it in the left hand, knot ten threads over it with the right hand; take the first two of these threads, and make six single chain; make three chain with the next two threads; take the next four threads, make a Solomon's knot, the same with tne next four threads: leave this for the present. Take up twelve threads, and with the last four of them make a Solomon's knot; make four single chain with each two of these threads; take the next four of them, hold the first in the right hand, knot each of the three threads on to it; with the left take the next four of them, hold the first thread in the right hand, knot nine threads on to it with the left; repeat for two more rows; take the first two of these threads, make three single chain. Do the same with the other six threads. Take one of the threads from the single chain at the left side, hold it in the right hand, knot eight threads on to it with the left; take up the other thread of the single chain, hold it in the right hand, knot eight threads on to it with the left, make two Solomon's knots with those eight threads. Take the fourth thread of the second Solomon's knot at the left side of this, hold it in the right hand, and knot four threads on to it with the left. Repeat for three more rows; take the top thread of these four rows, hold it in the left hand, knot the three threads over it; with the right hand then make a Solomon's knot with these four threads, and do the same with the other four threads, this forms a small medallion. Take four of these threads at the right side, and the four threads next to it; make another medallion; then make two Solomon's knots with the eight threads; then take the remaining four threads of the first medallion with the four threads next to it; make another medallion; then make two Solomon's knots with the eight threads; then take four threads of these, and four of the second medallion, and make another medallion; then make two Solomon's knots with the eight threads; take up the thread at the side of the third medallion, hold it in the right hand, knot eight threads on to it with the left; take the next thread, do the same; take these eight threads and with every two of them make three chain. Take up one thread of the single chain at the beginning, hold it in the right hand, knot eight threads over it; repeat for two more rows; take the two first threads of these, make six single chain; take the next four threads, hold the first in the right hand, knot three threads over it; loosen the fifth straight line, hold it in the right hand, knot each thread twice on to it with the left.

The remainder of the centre patterns can be made by following the engraving, as it is almost all a repetition of what has been described, and the pattern at the top is repeated at the bottom of

No. 16.

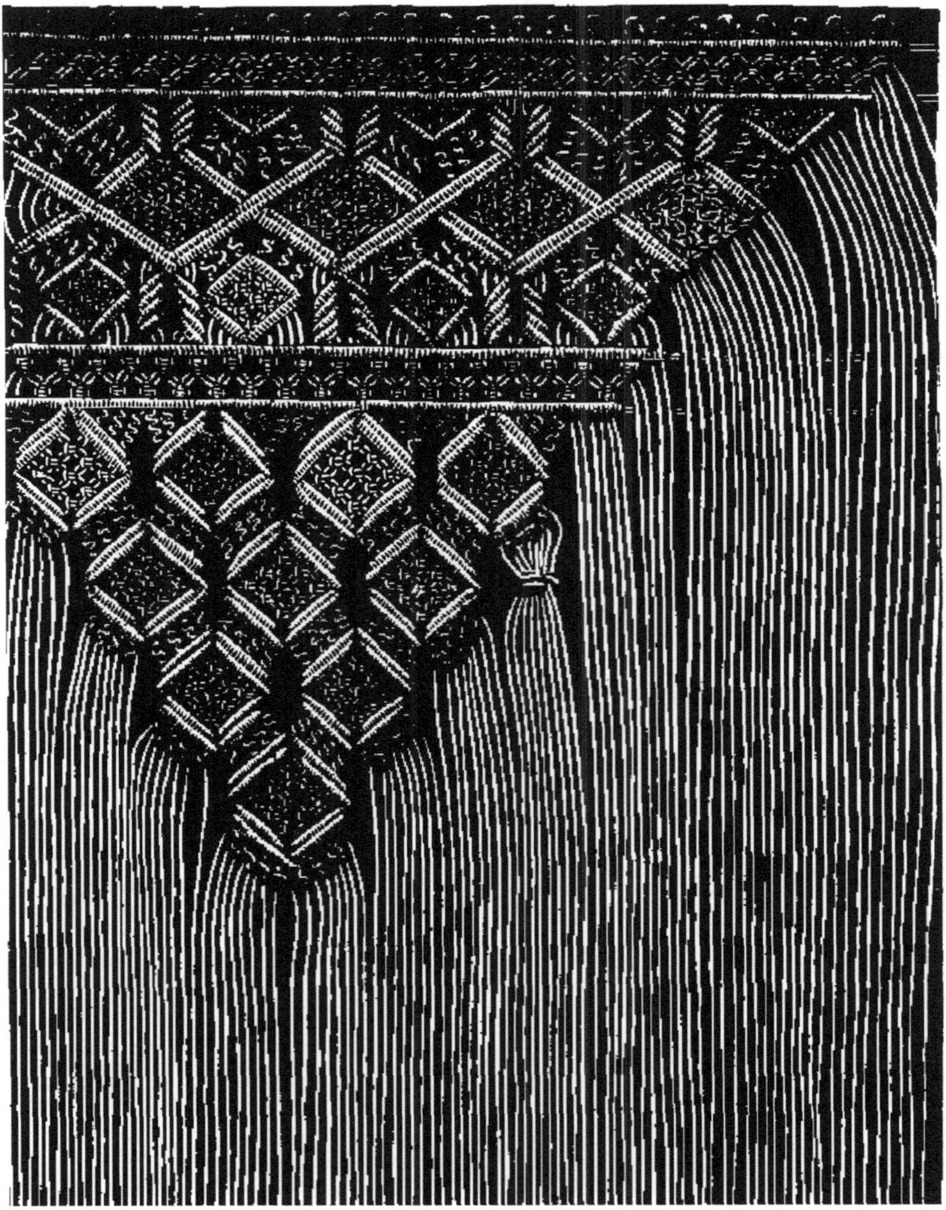

the Insertion, only reversing the order of working; and for fastening off the threads, *see* Instructions No. IV., Insertion Pattern.

No. 16.

(Threads for this Pattern two yards long).

Pin on the threads in the usual way to the cushion, and to make the Picot heading. Take two threads, hold the ends of them evenly together, then pin them on to the cushion above the first line, and make with them two double chain over the pin. Repeat to the end of cushion. Then loosen the first line at the right side, hold it in the right hand, and knot each thread twice on to it with the left; then make three rows of Solomon's knots to the end of cushion. Then loosen the second line, hold it in the right hand, knot each thread twice on to it with the left; take the first two threads, make eight chain; * take the next twelve threads, make three Solomon's knots; and under these make three more according to the engraving. Take the first of these twelve threads, hold it in the right hand, knot five threads on to it with the left; take the last of these twelve threads, hold it in the left hand, knot six threads on to it with the right; make five single chain with every two of these threads. Leave these for the present. Take up four threads; hold the first in the right hand, knot the three threads on to it with the left. Repeat for three more rows, to form a leaf. Take the next four threads, hold the fourth in the left hand, knot the three threads on with the right hand. Repeat for three more rows. Repeat from * to end of cushion Take up the second thread; hold it in the right hand, knot six threads on to it with the left hand; take up the first thread, knot six threads on in the same way. Take up the first thread of the first leaf, hold it in the left hand, knot six threads on to it with the right; take the next thread of the leaf, do the same. Then take the first leader at the left side, hold it in the right hand, and knot the first leader at the right side twice on to it; do the same with the other two leaders. Then under the two leaves, make a Solomon's knot with four threads, take the fourth thread of the second leaf, hold it in the right hand, knot six threads on to it with the left, take the remaining thread of the leaf, hold it in the right hand: do the same. Then with those sixteen threads make fifteen more Solomon's knots, making in all sixteen, take up the second leader at the left side, hold it in the right hand, knot eight threads on to it with the left; take up the first leader, and do the same; take the seventh thread, hold it in the left hand, knot the six threads on to it with the right; take up the eighth thread, hold it in the left hand, knot the seven threads on to it with the right hand; take the first two of these threads, make ten single chain; take the next two threads, make five single chain; do the same with the ten remaining threads; take the seventh thread, hold it in the left hand, knot the six threads over it with the right; take up the eighth thread, hold it in the right hand, knot five threads on to it with the left. Then with those twelve threads make nine Solomon's knots according to the engraving. Take up the first of these threads; hold it in the right hand, knot five threads on to it with the left, do the same on the other side, holding the leader in the left hand and knotting the threads on with the right. Repeat from * to the end of cushion. Then loosen the third straight line, hold it in the right hand, knot each thread on to it with the left. Then take four threads, make two Solomon's knots. Repeat to end. Miss two threads, take the next four threads make two Solomon's knots. Repeat to end. Loosen the fourth line, hold it in the right hand, knot each thread on to it with the left.

To Make the Scollop.—*Take the first two threads, make six single chain; take the next two threads, make four single chain; make two single chain with the next; take up two threads, hold the second in the left hand, knot seven threads over it with the right. Repeat for another row. Take up eight threads, make five chain with the last two of them; make four chain with the next, and two chain with the next; take up the first of these eight threads; hold it in the right hand, knot seven threads on to it with the left. Repeat for another row. Then with twelve of those threads make nine Solomon's knots according to the engraving. Then take up the first thread; hold it in the right hand; knot seven threads on to it with the left. Repeat for another row. Take the last thread; hold it in the left hand; knot seven threads on to it with the right. Repeat for another row. Then take the leader from the other side, and knot it twice on to this leader; then take the first of these threads, make three single chain, do the same with the next six threads; then miss the first thread; take the two next threads, and make three chain; do the same to the next two threads, and the same to the following two threads; then make six single chain with every two of the remaining eight threads; this forms a diamond. Repeat from * until there are ten diamonds, according to the engraving, to form the scollop.

No. 17.

(MATERIALS.—A weighted Cushion with German pins, and linen thread or silk.)

The lace is made by knotting the threads together, the rule to be observed being to take one thread as a leader, hold it firmly, and knot each single thread twice on to it, always keeping the leader at the top. When the leaf is worked from right to left, the leader is held in the left hand, and when the leaf is worked from left to right, the leader is held in the right hand.

Cut the cross lines the length of the lace required, fasten them on the cushion with the largest pins; the threads for this pattern are to be one yard four inches long.

INSTRUCTIONS.

Fasten the threads on as follows: Pass the two ends of each thread under the first line, pointing them up, then draw them back through the loop. Then put in a pin between every four threads. Loosen the second line at the right side, hold it in the right hand, and knot each thread twice on to it with the left hand.

First line of open work: Take the first four threads, hold three in the left hand, and knot the fourth thread three times over them with the right hand; so on to the end. Then take two threads from each, hold three in the right hand and knot the fourth three times over them with the left hand. Then loosen the third line, hold it in the right hand and knot each thread twice on to it.

To make the first leaf: Take eight threads, hold the eighth one in the left hand as leader, knot each of the seven threads twice on to it

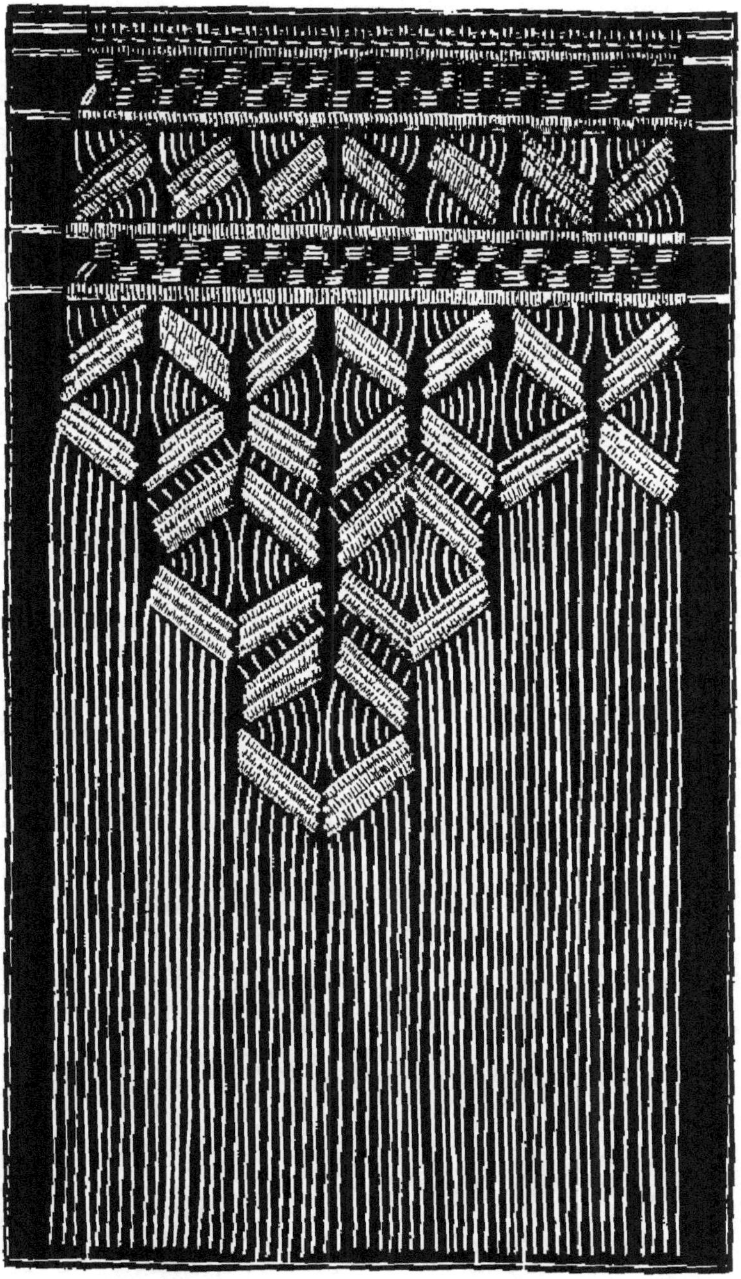

with the right hand, always keeping the leader at the top and the threads underneath. Then the eighth again, hold it in the left hand and knot the seven threads twice on to it with the right; the third line of the leaf is made in the same way, repeat for the second and third leaf. Fourth leaf: hold the thread at the left side in the right hand as leader, and knot the threads on to it with the left hand. Then take the fourth line and knot each thread twice on to it in the same way; second line of open work same as the first, then take the fifth line and knot each thread twice on to it.

First leaf of scollop: take eight threads, hold the eighth one in the left hand as leader, and make the leaf same as the first one in the insertion.

When this leaf is finished, pass the leader to the right hand and make a second leaf. Third leaf: hold the leader in the right hand and knot on the threads with the left. Fourth leaf: pass the leader of the third leaf to the left hand, and knot on the threads with the right hand. When this leaf is finished, knot the leader twice on to the leader of the second leaf. The remainder of the scollop is made in the same way, as may be seen by the engraving.

CPSIA information can be obtained
at www.ICGtesting.com
Printed in the USA
BVHW040951041020
590249BV00007B/568

9 780343 878184